PERDIDO

T0307136

PERDIDO

Elaine Terranova

Grid Books BOSTON

Off the Grid Press is an imprint of Grid Books.

GRID BOOKS, Boston, MA
www.grid-books.org

Copyright © 2018, by Elaine Terranova.
Cover illustration copyright © 2017 by Sara Eichner.
All rights reserved.

FRONT COVER
64 layers, red and orange split (detail),
pen and ink drawing, 2017, by Sara Eichner.

Printed by Thomson-Shore, Dexter, Michigan.

ISBN: 978-1-946830-02-9

perdido: *p.p. & adj.* lost; strayed; mislaid; ruined

The University of Chicago Spanish-English/English-Spanish Dictionary

"Perdido" is a driving composition in the popular A-A-B-A form. Its simplicity, short phrases, and irresistible swing feeling have made it one of the top vehicles for jazz jam sessions. As a result, recordings of "Perdido" are frequently ten minutes or more in length, allowing for multiple instrumental solos and variations on the basic theme.

The Complete Jazz at the Philharmonic on Verve 1944–1949

There is a parable—or maybe it's just part of a stand-up routine— that at the end of your life you are reunited with all the things that you have lost in your life.

GEOFF DYER, *Zona: A Book About a Film About a Journey to a Room*

In loving memory of my friends:

Russell Astley

Nina Auerbach

Henry Braun

Dorothea Grossman

Joan Landis

Frank Moore

CONTENTS

PERDIDO

Wedding Cento

—Lines taken from *Into the Garden: A Wedding Anthology*
edited by Robert Hass and Stephen Mitchell

I have come into my garden.
Though green leaves only witness,
my heart is like a singing bird.

Now touch the air softly.
I would like to watch you sleeping.
Now you will feel no rain.

Marriage is in many ways
a simplification of life.
Here all seeking is over.

Let us lose sight of ourselves
and break the mirrors. Turn me
like a waterwheel turning a millstone.

Loving is a journey with water and stars.
O you tender ones, walk now.
Don't run anymore. Quiet.
How pure the hearts of lovers as they walk.
How softly it rains.

I THE GARDEN

Moon Jar

Celestial vessel
seamlessly seamed,
two hemispheres sealed
as earth is sealed to sky,

a white crystallization
purposed to catch
and hold the moon.

Vessel perfected
by imperfection
with its underglaze of blue,
run of dawn-pink.

I see night's swell
drawn up in it,
heart swell,
rival to
my own anticipation.

Oh, let the moon tide me
wherever it spills,
whatever its path,
its downward thrust,

the moon jar's thirst.

Palm Beach

What did I see?

I saw the island, its finality,
the sun beating on the water.
An orange ball roll toward me
in the pool.

A chain of pelicans passed overhead
metallic and intricate,
clenched in Escher circles.

I saw the gecko and the snake
and at the bonsai garden,
ficus, serenissima,
in training since late last century.

I stood alone on a sidewalk
as noon struck
and had to cross
to a safe shadow of roofs

while all along, moist warmth
like human breath
licked at the v's of my fingers.

Mimosa

Pink aureoles peek through
a fringe of leaves.
The scent, the bright
excitement
arouses the hummingbird.

Once I changed
into my bathing suit
in the back seat of a car
as a man pointed it out to me.
"Mimosa," he said. "It means Beloved."

Hummingbird

What with foresight and dancing,
gypsies pass easily
between worlds. The hummingbird too—

only a moth with a beak—
have I ever heard it hum?

Yet it's everywhere welcome,
coaxed by red flowers, even sugar water,
for we are devious in our desires.

And the dead, we embody them
for our own purposes. I can't talk
to a shadow, to an abstraction.

A sun worshiper, my brother,
always raising his face to it.
One touch and the body roar quieted.

Today, though I walk the length
of the park he is not there.
He is nowhere under the sun.

I want the dead but am beside
the living. The tulips throw up their hands.
The lunch crowd swallows me.

Renoir, "le Pêcheur à la Ligne"

A couple pass
their Sunday by a stream.
A net of sunlight settles over them.

The young man rests one arm
in back of him
and with the other
guides a fishing pole.

Birdlike, some feet away,
the woman bends
toward an embroidery.

So undisturbed they are, so still,
leaves reach for them
and living forms turn toward them
in the grass.

They do not speak,
shaped to their tasks, not work
but a slow, sensual mastery,

both moving with the stream
in the same diagonal line
of culmination.

Shadow

As if alive,
leaf shadow trembles
in its dark projection
onto the deck,
all movement and diminishment.

It flinches like thread
I hold to the needle's eye.
Like a butterfly shaken loose
by wind from the throat of a lily.
Like a sigh dispersing
the withheld breath.

Motet

After my slow recovery from night
I wake and let my body
warm to room temperature,

my gaze filled with outside, pines
and the gaping world.

A dream
lifting like a cloud,
the breath of day
up against my face.

Have I ever been kissed
with so much attention?

All night I swatted butterflies
by the dim light of sleep.
Where was the chink
in the air-tight house? Sky
that jettisoned them?

Click of turquoise and gold
metallic wings as they hit the wall,
at which point they softened
and opened into bows.

Embedded

In the dark, it's safe to move around.
By day you will be seen, though nature
offers its disguises, the spice bush
that shelters deer and matched to a leaf,
a smiling swallowtail caterpillar.

The sun sculpts turf around you,
quiet, translucent grasses
and skunk cabbage you will be lost among.

Crouch against outcroppings of rock
you can shape yourself to,
or self-shadow, as the turkey vulture does,
drawing itself into itself, in the fields.

The Shattered House

—after a drawing of van Ruisdael

Sometimes stars fall into a planet,
not the other way around,
space debris like the Perseids
that shower our hillside,
the sparkle of salt thrown
over the shoulder for good luck.

They move as leaves move
across my field of vision
or it may be just the shadow
of leaves I see, blowing
in the wind of my eyelashes.

I can just make out
the shattered house here, where
the road stops short,
bare slanted boards falling in
on darkness while sunlight
taps at the rest of the world.

Left Fork

Along the road big trees lie upended
while slender ones flex their necks, rearing up
like deer. And where do you look for light
in a sky that detaches from sky as fog,

day just breaking? You look down
the roadbank to the open face of the stream
though here boys roll old tires, dark ciphers
that land where smashed cans flash. Farther on,

still pristine, the stream has dug a hollow
below the lumberyard, a slow path
hunters or poachers follow, once leaves
begin their cover-up. It's where that noon

the shining wand of a shotgun
on the seat beside him, the suicide turned in,
hearing, as I do now, the heartbeat
of the wind ping through the guardrail.

II HISTORY

Awake

Last night I dreamed I was awake. An excess of conscious-
ness, maybe. I dreamed I was in a war. Wars presently are
fought in deserts though how can there be a war in a desert?
You have to hide behind trees in a war. Or maybe that's only
tag. I dreamed one army was cutting branches from the tree
in front of the house and wood was flying in through the
window. The blanket weighed down my bones. I dreamed
there was a sleeping boy in my lap and I couldn't rouse him.

History

In the courtyard, a flock of 40 parrots
returns as arabesques of smoke rise
through the pierced copper lanterns.

Earlier, it seems in some other century,
we ran with our children
under the bridge to avoid the shooting,

believing as we ran that repetition
of a single name is a path to survival. And after,
I saw we were fine, we were sound.

I saw we could be doing these same things,
sipping tea, turning the pages of a book,
with bullets flying through windows.

We could be basking in sunlight
while over us fell the shadow of tanks,
waiting for life to resume or waiting
as our torn bodies remembered to bleed.

I Remember What a Drone Once Was

That it was Allen Ginsberg,
thumbing the key of his harmonium

to invoke Wm. Blake,
songs trimmed on the page with triangular
angel wings.

That it started with
the eyes of mica winking in the dark

as I watched Ginsberg
hold the key down, electrified,
doorbell pressed forever

in the natural stone amphitheater
of Upper Black Eddy, Bucks County.

I'd spent hours picking a dress,
even put up my hair—

Oh, I know I didn't need to,
that it would be a dim walk through pines
to get to that place

that I might and I did snag my stockings
and a spider web as well, which hung
suspended from the boughs,
and have to rough through it a door.

Seated beside me, who were they?
Those people in the mind's dark theater

where you'd know faces only
by the brush of your hand.

I'd thought a drone
was a bee, was a motorcycle vroom,
or overpowering alarm,

I didn't know what.
The sound came to us
like a prolonged cough, like the amplified
turning of a stubborn jar

until it was no longer loud
until I could pull my hands away from my ears

and it became an om,
continuing tone of the universe.

The Day

It was the day the earth caught fire,
the longest day, the day summer arrived,
8 o'clock sharp in the evening. The sounds,
the expectation I experienced, waiting.
It was the end of books, the end of end papers
and closure. Covers snapped like a trap,
yet everyone was writing a book.
And the war went on as wars go on.
The number down grew. It was the day
the earth caught fire but the birds didn't know
before it was too late. They called to one another
from various trees, cherry, beech, ash, still seeking
a connection. And insects proceeded,
drunken, erratic, their paths deflected
by enveloping heat. It was the day the earth
caught fire and the troops staggered on broken roads
and the temperature of the sand rose until
it was molten glass. The uniforms mocked the desert
and the desert cracked under heaving tanks
while here, a mockingbird recycled his repertoire
of whistles, warbles, sequenced like a car alarm
going off. We listened, rapt. It was the day the earth
caught fire and the stars would not show themselves again.

Samurai Sword

Priceless.
Sometimes 1,000 years old
and tested on at least two corpses.
Museum quality, one able
to penetrate five bodies at once.

Designed to pierce
the boiled leather armor
of the Monguls
as they came up
out of the sea at Kamakura—
a typhoon, a divine wind.

Worn cutting edge up,
only a single motion required
to withdraw it and strike.

Black clay firmed the edge,
red clay, the interior.
It would be fired a dozen times
and quenched in cold water
to temper the metal,
to bake a hardness
into its heart.

Hammering freed it
of impurities,
crystalline particles
that might dim
the *ka*, wavy line near the edge,
pattern of clouds or rays of the sun.

The polisher, *togishi*,
glazed it until the steel
was a mirror.
He had to rid himself of ego
for the sword's sake,
heels cradled on wood blocks
to stop his inching forward.

He'd pick up a coarse grindstone
to start then smooth stones,
each smaller than the last,
to dispatch rough edges
and scratches,

finishing with a tiny,
delicate file the shape
of a flower petal.

The Lean Horse, and the Fat

Head down, belly drooping.
Backbone raking hide.

It's envy I fix on.
Success, I don't have the stomach for it.

Where the fat horse, headstrong and sleek,
pulls away with his bridle,
I follow, circumspect, a razor of want,

the next step and the next,
over a yellow ground of sun
or hoof dust.
We go at least in the same direction,

invention of Ren Renfa,
also known as Taoist on Moon Mountain
and White Cloud Fisherman.

A court scene captures him,
thin supplicant in a black robe,
bowing to the rotund Kublai Khan.

Ren, painter of the Yuan,
though it felt to him like the Tang,
pure literati, as he smoothed color over silk.

Silk feeling, I know it,
the pull of silk along flank,
closest I will come to heaven.

Hikikomori

—young people in Japan, self-willed shut-ins

I don't think you should go out
while the weather is uncertain.

Or maybe just to the place
where trees grow so thick
even wind can't get through.

No one would find you there
for ages. Aokigahora, "sea
of trees," as if in it you'd drown.

And why go out at all
when there is no guarantee
of safety? In the room where I sleep

I have a window I keep shuttered
and a video screen.

My parents bring me trays
and try to speak
but I plead something holy,
meditation, like an orange
being peeled from the inside.

Picture, 1950

The picture caught me
in a red dress that held me
like a sausage casing.

It caught me with my mother's
wide cheeks
barely closing on what might be
a grasshopper but is probably
only my overbite,
caged teeth that don't meet.

(A picture
is heartless, a picture is
so one-sided.)

This is about myself
but not exactly,
about myself
half-turned away.

The picture caught me
squeezed up in a laugh
of embarrassment. My eyes are there
but where are they
directed?

It caught me like
the wiry hair clipped to my skull
with a bobby pin.

It caught me in worn saddle shoes
wavy in the soles

as I perched
on the low cement rampart
that set off a flower bed.

The camera had a stronger
gravity than the sun.

The picture caught me forever,
in that box brownie
wielded by the neighborhood druggist,
perv for little girls.

It caught me and I waited
but no matter how many times I passed,
I never showed up

with the pretty girls
in the drug store window
behind the glass wall of day.

The Measure

I came in the morning to the fiber lab
where I stacked liquid-saturated strands
with calipers onto the pans of fine scales.
The chemist, my boss, stood behind,
interrupting my concentration with his nervous,
vocal swallowing. Otherwise, there'd be only
the dream state of my calibrations
and the ticking, seething machines. Something
always on the boil. That's how I remember
myself, balanced between child and adult.
A first job, my clumsy fingers. The white lab coat
I wore as a disguise. The care I took, and yet
values I could never corroborate.

I ate my sandwich seated on the same high stool,
then took a short lunchtime walk to monitor autumn,
to stack against it other autumns, decide
what was nature, what, like who you'd love,
if not exactly choice, at least beyond helping.
Already we'd turned back the clock so the dark
could come sooner. Childhood was a fairy tale
I whispered to myself as I fell asleep. I couldn't
yet commit to a future, take between then
and now a side.

                    Back in the warmth after lunch
I plied the scale again with an airy gold of filaments.
Then I made my more or less careful measurements,
the pans unsettling like feathers in wind.

Etiology of the Migraine

1. Definition

Megrim:
"Pain in half the head."

2. Triggers

Sound that splinters still air:
the struck gong.

In an incandescent bulb,
filament glowing
like an upside down question mark.

Sun
and motes of dust outlined
by sun.

3. Visual Presentation

Tracking a bat
across the ceiling. First the bat,
then its shadow

or first the shadow, then the bat.

The dazzle of diamonds
flipped between the palms.

The 4,500 twitching mosquitoes
a brown bat
can ingest in a night.

4. *Course*

An artery swells,
pulses in one temple.

The view tilts, strain
as you do to right it,
the bowl of peaches
wobbling out of reach,
books and pens, round-backed chairs
and table.

First, a shiver,
the frisson of knowing.
An instant of vertigo

before the forehead shrinks
to bone and pain.

5. *Anecdotal Evidence*

For a long while I wake every day
at 7:26, that's how
the slats of digital numbers fall,

address of my father's shop
where on a lathe he rhythmically cut facets
into the irregular rockface of a diamond.

Then day proceeds,
studded with seconds.

6. *Consequence*

Each migraine
leaves a tiny scar in the brain.

7. *Known Cures*

Sugar.

Darkness.

Persephone in the Dark

Sun slips behind cloud. How easy then
for a girl to be misled, plucked out of the quiet,
out of the thicket. Out of summer itself
by a bandit or god. Lost from the field
or quirk in a road's turning.

He throws his voice ahead of him.
His breath at last on the long
girl neck—
a man too old, too finished for her,
who'd never let her
be who she was.

Everything stopped,
the green world grows still,
leaving off.

I saw a narcissus I couldn't reach,
otherwise, rock gardens
that seemed to be growing
only rock.

Where I walked, the road
whitened and then went to shadow.
Rabbits withdrew.
Snakes shivered back into crevices.

Left or right, I forgot to look
only carried away
what was already inside.

I no longer remember
if this
was my life
or my mother's,

only the wandering god,
a little menacing
like Ezio Pinza in South Pacific.

His performance:
she loved the way he clung
to the piano, one foot en pointe,
and when he once needed
a music stand for the score
and when he once forgot the words
like a bashful suitor.

Strength, I wanted,
to be protected,
whether it was my mother
or whoever loved me.

Seal up the house, she'd say,
seal it so nothing can get in.

But always the weight piled up,
seesawed between
what needs to go out,
garbage, the cat, myself,
what wants to come in.

And sneaking off,
something I'd find,

a pimple or a tear in my blouse,
to counterweight the happiness.

Of course, I'd come back—
where else would I go?
Silence and cold,
the anger of crows,
when nothing grew,
which was the story of winter.

Cell Call, One Side

He said:

"Did you have to call me here?..."

"It's just, you're so clinging..."

"But I do love you..."

"Did you say you packed my things?..."

"What did you hear about me?..."

"Anyway, I don't think you can live
a single day without me."

"Quilt Made by Carrie Bonivul Thomas or her Mother or her Aunt"

Nothing passed through her house
that wasn't of use. Nothing passed
through her hands that didn't have potential.
She could see it, from the man's
corduroy trousers her son outgrew
to the gingham shirt, collar already twice turned.
Nothing in this life that couldn't find
fulfillment in another form. Sunday jacket,
what remained around the tear,
pieced and shaped and stuffed into a bag
under the stair. And whether the made quilt
was hers or her mother's or her aunt's,
like the "Love, precious love," trills and harmonies
they traded, could she claim it?
Sewing with kin into early morning,
anyone's fingers taking the tiny, necessary stitches
so no one of their blood need lie
exposed to night, uncovered by their love.

Keeper

"It was difficult to make out precisely what was in the heap
for the dust lay on it so thick that the hands of anyone who
touched it at once looked like gloves." —*Dead Souls,* Gogol

Crows clear their throats
in preparation: another day
of rummaging.

It's raining and buds rain,
wisteria or whatever it is
rising in back of me

while soaked men
heft like Sisyphus
huge cans of stuff into
a gaping garbage truck.

Some time, could it be possible?
Nothing will be left
that is still me.

But a keeper keeps,
and here inside,
despite the grime and flies,
my vista is an Alp of magazines,

slivered soap and pencil stubs,
scraps that flutter
orchid-like in wind.

To rub each surface
for its genie, clean,
just slows the groping dust.

I could, of course, pick up,
pick up at least and leave
the mess behind.
Sporca. Pig! you'd say.

Whatever enters here, you'd say,
sinks into the quicksand
of oblivion: doorknobs,
the sole of a shoe.
But an object waits,
that is its nature.
I wouldn't want
to grieve for one lost thing.

Plastic

To get rid of it, he put the plastic into the wood stove fire. No, I told him. It was the plastic center of the cardboard pie box. Tear off the plastic first, I said. It winged my nose. My leg began to swell. My hair pricked. Don't, I told him. It could only burn as itself, unnaturally. It wasn't natural. (See, my neck won't turn, I said.) Not burn the way the rest of the pie box burned. It smoked my lungs. Not eagerly as the rest of the cardboard pie box burned. But it couldn't stop itself entirely, any more than the birds outside could stop calling after each other when it got dark. I breathed it in, plastic eye that uncovered the pie. I swallowed it, the pie eye, center that looked down into the pie through the top of the cardboard pie box top. It feathered in the fire into ash. NO, I told him. My temples pushed inward to meet in the center of my skull as a plastic acrid bird of fire lifted into the air.

Goodbye, Sofabed

Last night I sat for the last time
in the lap
of the 27-year-old sofabed,
its age, the age
of our marriage.

Platform
for whatever love was made
while we waited
for a bed
to turn the room overhead
into a bedroom

though the hidden, thin mattress
never fit
any sheet I owned.

The cover was
a Rorschach of stains and tears
I knew like my own skin,

and all along,
hollows and bumps
where it caved to countless rumps.

But that sofabed had its charm.
Once an overnight guest
woke to find a cat she hadn't put there
tucked under her arm.

And there were festive traces
of New Years
and early-on ambitious dinner party fare,
chocolat pots de crème,
pissaladière.

Did I say flowered white chintz
had doomed it from the start?

Yet a nice match
for the green Queen Anne chair
an upholsterer's apprentice wrapped in mohair,
unable to tame
its sharp springs.

When I complained he struck back,
I recall,
"That flowered couch
clashes with your wall."

And if he was right?
But I told him—it was the sofa I defended—
that no, it blended.

And it mostly did.
Mostly.
Mostly it will be how my mind,
looking back,
furnishes
this room, this house, this life.

III EXCHANGES

Actors

The actor tears off the mask of ordinary life. His face shakes out side to side, a laugh that is not glee. His real eyes burn through the dark.

A squiggle of red greasepaint, maybe lipstick, works its way down from his forehead along the neck to arm and forearm. It travels the path of an artery, life blood unraveling on the outside of the body. The actor shrugs and the red route skillfully deviates.

A muscle in the torso moves, a little flap, another. Each is the seat of deep emotion. A Reichian could press and the stifled feeling break through into a scream, reconstituting shame or a slap or a parent's silent displeasure.

The actor punches against the box of the proscenium, attacking empty, auxiliary space. The only escape, a window painted on a scrim. Slap, slap of his feet on the stage as they run in place, path to nowhere.

The actor mimics us, he echoes what we say. His mouth opens in a red-rimmed O, enclosing horror or sorrow. Let us not forget despair, which the actor recreates, the ragged edges of anyone's hunger.

In chorus, the group of actors arrive at what we are thinking, mouthing it, sometimes without words. They sit in a line like rowers, legs gripping the haunches of the body in front, white and dark triangles of light describe on their faces the plates of the skull.

The actors throw off their ragged suit jackets which fall at their feet and then bare-chested, they too sink to the floor. They crawl, they draw themselves up like caterpillars, stretching and squeezing, pulling together top and bottom ends. They bend and scrub, scrub a circle with the discarded cloth in an effort to polish or purify the fundament.

The actors toil. They spit and sweat. They cry. In the dark, a spotlight glares and they appear to liquefy. I myself no longer cry. There is a lock on my grief.

The actress makes of her face a moonscape, planetary. There is strain in the neck, a head is heavy to uphold. A shudder passes across her visage, tremor traversing a bowl of milk. Her elbows lift up like batwings.

Chamber Society

Tonight at the concert, where I knew
virtually everyone in the audience,
the cellist attacked her instrument

self-absorbed like a silent movie star,
all trial and peril, young forehead
wrinkling, eyes encased in black

and the bow split hairs and the pianist
with concern looked on, depressing
the shining white keys with a click
like chalk dropped to a tabletop

while the hall, with our knees drawn up
to accommodate the previous row's press,
was heated mainly with our breath.

An audience I had lived among
what seemed centuries, any one of whom
might even tonight die of hearing
Beethoven, or Bach, or Rachmaninoff.

I sat in my own mad throes of listening
until the soloist, ravaged and spent,
and her elegant, solicitous accompanist
left the stage, trailed by the self-effacing turner.

Stone

I went to the graveyard where they lay, my parents,
but didn't look for them. All the family rested here
after they'd finished living, as they might at the end
of a heavy meal. Instead, I found myself
in my brother's plot, a headstone being unveiled.
The stone bore his name, I could see, having already
shrugged off its shawl of lace. And though I'd left
a smaller stone on top to say I'd been, as others had,
it was the living I was there for, my nephew who chanted
Yisgodol, v'yiskadash, the Hebrew prayer, in the same
appropriate monotone the rabbi used to usher his father
into eternity, and my niece and her daughters stood by,
pretty shadows in black mini funeral dresses
and sunglasses. The stones went back and back,
straight shouldered in rows, soldiers of death. I myself
didn't want it to be known where I'd lie, even here
    among family,
just return to the atmosphere as if I had evaporated.

Unsent Letter to Dottie in L.A.

It's California here,
almost. October and seventy degrees.
Golden, my street. A smoke of yellow leaves,
color of the sunny room that stood
for day in my daydream.

More and more of what I want to say
gets crammed into the empty space of margins.
I couldn't read the words myself.

Do you remember leaves
I once dropped into an envelope—
an urgent telegram
of autumn—instead of any letter?

I sat with the leaf pile and sorted,
on one side, those with something to say,
dull rust of the mute ones
that rubbed together into nothing
on the other. Thinking what you passed
on that journey across,

golf courses, a foretaste of paradise,
the moon calling out
to the water, "Come."

The Monarchs should be where you are by now
on their way to Mexico with other
blue chip butterflies.

Here, not even crickets are left
to pluck at the air at night.

Death came at me

on a motorcycle
into the intersection at 60 miles per
with no helmet
arms open,
legs branching.

Ahead I saw him,
and then behind
in the rearview, where he had
completed the turn,
separate
from his simple machine,
sheen of red on asphalt.

And wasn't that death, too,
halting but deliberate,
death, unmistakable,
approaching our fancy,
outdoor lunch
as my friend tapped out her troubles:
    not good
    no more
    not again,
—which was her life—
with a teaspoon on the table.

I wouldn't look up, wouldn't give
the dollar's worth
of attention he demanded,

something to eat. But I found him
again, later, another day, taste
of morning, steel in my mouth,

Death, advancing
at the same
ceremonial pace.

Junk

Junk, what she took with her
from drawers that barely shut
on photographs, knives, melted
rubber bands, all of it
she traded for new as soon as she could.
But then she came back.

They went to the same
flea market on Sundays and rubbed
cheap glass or looked into
old *Life* magazines.
Back home they lay on the bed
in dark sun and made love
the old way, so easy, without
disarranging themselves, without
opening their eyes.

                    Once,
square by square, they put down
a new kitchen floor, white tile
then black, white, black.
It made her lightheaded,
there was no firm ground.
That year they hung a Christmas tree
with candy wrappers, broken
necklaces, the way they got their sparkles.

They took in a homeless dog
when friends split,
though that should have given him
twice as many chances to be saved.

Woofer or Whopper, the name
a kid gave him. Their cat
jumped out of a window and under
a car when he came, flattening
to just the picture of a cat
she had to pass every day
as he dragged her along, making
little choking sounds, she walked
so slow. At night she was alone
and he battered his head
on the bedframe to get under.
His dark, curly hide
hid all that had gone wrong.

Suckling

There I was, suckling a baby. It wasn't my baby for I never had one. I had borrowed it from someone seated behind me, a big woman in a periwinkle coat. She said when she was away from the baby, her chest grew wet just with the thought of it. But the baby took to me right away. It rooted around like a pig and found my right nipple. It was a fat baby, a girl baby, skin just the color of my skin, so it blended and its flesh became a piece of my flesh. I felt the tiny mouth applied. I felt the warm stream of liquid draw through my breast. I wouldn't easily be able to separate again that baby from the rest of me if the mother wanted it back.

The Birth and Death and Birth of Ganesh

Parvati breathed into a doll she made from soap, and he came to life. That was Ganesh and when he wouldn't open the door to his father, Shiva, they fought. Shiva lopped off his head but immediately regretted it. He asked Brahma what could he do and was told, "That head is gone. You must find another, the head of the first living creature you see facing north, to put in its place." It turned out an elephant lay dying outside in the road. So Ganesh, pot-bellied remover of obstacles, lived on, half-God, with the head of an elephant, in his pretty, jeweled circus suit, as his mother's companion and amanuensis.

Ah, I remember, once before, someone came to life, *purusa*, a person. The creator, refining, separating the atmosphere, brought forth living creatures. Thus Parvati, without Shiva, without husband, set about making a creature for herself out of the discarded impurities of her own body, hardened in the Ganges.

Or maybe she did carve her small creature out of a bar of soap, the size of a quarter pound of butter, slippery in the river water, noting where the smile started, how the planes of the face might arrange themselves. Shaping a breath, "Come to me," she said, "come alive, something," and breathed into the tiny opening so like a mouth. And as spring rises up from the ground in forsythia, golden exhalations, Ganesh breathed out and came alive.

From then, it is by now a very long day. It is stretching into centuries. Ganesh told Parvati, "Dead, I dreamed I was awake, and I woke alive." True, left alone in the house, he did not know Shiva and staunch as an iron gate, barred the way. But what child knows his father for sure, or father his son? Anyhow, Shiva was always looking on the dark side. "Although Shiva beheaded me," Ganesh said, "he couldn't kill me since it was my mother alone who made me, and forever I remain at her side."

Walk, Memorial Day

Summer St.
The flagged houses.
The orange cat I frighten.
The tick of sprinklers.
The picket fences.
The dried bouquet tossed on a lawn.
The sun at eye level.
The homeowner pruning boxwood.
The cellophaned door.
The essence of jasmine.
The anthills, the ants.
The wrong turn. The cars.
The mental health banner.
The churches. The market.
The streets that go uphill.
The streets that go back.
Summer St.
The same orange cat
on the opposite side.
The charcoal grilling.
The stranger passing
who calls out, "Smells good!"
The path of impatiens.
The tripartite birches.
The snatches of song.
The tree house. Its ladder.
The rhododendrons
balled up like fists.
The drooping branches.
The quiet, clinging.
The evening.

Perdido

It's snowing and all that's
behind us is lost: the yard
where a whining dog is chained

and the next one
that a boy sits in to pluck guitar notes
out of the gelid air of summer nights.

All I touch softly with my eyes
has slid into oblivion.

When my husband
goes out to shovel the walk
I'm afraid
he won't find the way to shovel
himself in again.

Then it's morning of another day
or it could be
the same day continuing.

I see his hair has been clipped so close
it might be a penance,
the head, a mossed stone.

*

Snow, and everything is white,
the color of absence.

Then, out front, a starling moment,
or not starlings,
just lostlings on their way somewhere,

trim brown birds
who set down
in the hostile territory of cold, fleshing out
the bones of trees, chirping away
like children.

An ambulance
flashes its tiara of red and blue lights,
Christmas in extremis,
stretching out for someone
a milk-white
stretcher.

Not the generic dead,
this one is known.
Not the generic siren
but one that comes bleating
like an entire flock.

*

I never touched my family in any intimate way
except as they lay dying.
Even then, I couldn't put my lips
to my brother Leo's cracked, bleeding lips,

only brushed back Sidney's
once-black hair,
sealing his forehead with a kiss.
Youngest, I'd been born
for this,

to be a good steward,
take care of what grows beside you,
what you must watch die.

*

I love that song, "Perdido."
It goes on, it seems, forever.
Pi-like, like repeating decimals.
It has, I tell you, the ping of forever.

I once knew a man called Peditto,
For years, I thought that his name
was Perdido. He read poems
at North Star on Mondays,
a neighborhood bar on Fairmont.

Maybe he also played sax there.
Music like spilled wine
had soaked into the floor boards.

*

At night, for protection, I curl up
into myself in sleep,
the way stars and planets
draw into a ball.
(There are no sharp corners in space.)

I'm a simple creature,
not extravagant or complex
like an elephant,

no extendable appendage
to brag of
for lifting and setting a thing down,
for trumpeting into a dark wood
or crowding any other
idea out of a room.

I have, what I'm saying,
no particular specialization, nothing
past a shoulder, an elbow, a hip,
though I can only ever see myself
from the shoulders down.

*

Sometimes in spring, rain like a chain
holds me back.
From inside, I hear it
gallop up the street.

It runs by like a river,
wanting nothing
but for you
to wash your feet in it.

Once after a great storm
I found sheltered in my basement
a long slug without a shell
(it had the shape of a boomerang),
a dead baby bat,
the rusted dinner knife
I'd searched for, for days,
all of which made me think of a place
I pass each day on the bus:
Laboratory for Research
into the Unreliability of Matter.

Witness

A tiny click
like the snap of fingers
precipitates
an explosion of music

or the louvre door
to the foyer
slams to,
before the outside door
even thinks
of crashing closed.

Noise leaves,
noise
which has
become our witness

until the time
one of us
goes out with it and is gone,
gone,
quiet following.

ACKNOWLEDGMENTS

The following poems appeared in or are forthcoming from these magazines, sometimes in slightly different form:

"Actor's," *Blue Lyra Review*
"Death Came at Me," *Per Contra*
"Embedded," *Salamander*
"Goodbye, Sofabed"; "Keeper," *Poetry South*
"Hikikomori"; "Shadow," *Cincinnati Review*
"History," *West Branch*
"Junk"; "Picture, 1950"; "Quilt Made by Carrie Bonivul Thomas
    or Her Mother or Her Aunt," *Women's Review of Books*
"Palm Beach," *5 a.m.*
"Persephone in the Dark," *Elegiac: Footnotes to Rilke's Duino Elegies*
    (chapbook)
"Plastic"; "Awake," *Hotel Amerika*
"The Day," *Apiary*

"Wedding Cento" was written for the wedding of Rhoda Kanevsky
    and Ray Kaplan

"The Shattered House" is dedicated to Samantha Block,
    student of science.

"Unsent Letter to Dottie" is dedicated to the poet,
    Dorothea Grossman, 1937–2012.

"Actors" derives from the work of the great Greek
    theater director, Theodoros Terzopoulos.

"The Lean Horse, and the Fat" was inspired by an
    ancient Chinese painting.

"Perdido," the song as I remember it, performed by
    saxophonist Ben Webster.

ELAINE TERRANOVA has published six collections of poems, most recently *Dollhouse*, which won the 2013 Off the Grid Poetry Prize, and two chapbooks. Her poems and prose have appeared in a number of literary magazines and anthologies and her translation of Euripides' *Iphigenia at Aulis* was published by the Penn Greek Drama Series. Her awards include grants from the Pennsylvania Council on the Arts, the Walt Whitman Award, NEA and Pew fellowships, and a Pushcart Prize. She is presently working on a childhood memoir.